CW00498681

Alcohol treatment services

A briefing by the National Audit Office

Report by the Comptroller and Auditor General

Ordered by the House of Commons
to be printed on 21 February 2023

This report has been prepared under Section 6 of the National Audit Act 1983 for presentation to the House of Commons in accordance with Section 9 of the Act

Gareth Davies
Comptroller and Auditor General
National Audit Office

16 February 2023

HC 1129 | £10.00

013594 02/23 NAO

Contents

This report can be found on the National Audit Office website at www.nao.org.uk

If you need a version of this report in an alternative format for accessibility reasons, or any of the figures in a different format, contact the NAO at enquiries@nao.org.uk

The National Audit Office study team consisted of:

Joanna Lewis,
Sophie McCammond,
Shivam Sood and
Janushanth Sritharan under the direction of Ashley McDougall.

For further information about the National Audit Office please contact:

National Audit Office
Press Office
157–197 Buckingham Palace Road
Victoria
London
SW1W 9SP

020 7798 7400

www.nao.org.uk

@NAOorguk

Key facts

602,000

government estimate of the number of people in England dependent on alcohol in 2018-19

£221mn

amount local authorities in England reported spending on alcohol treatment and prevention services in the community in 2021-22

84,697

people receiving treatment for alcohol only (and no other substances) in local authority treatment services in England in 2021-22

201 days average duration of treatment for people successfully completing treatment services for alcohol only (and no other substances) in 2021-22

98% proportion of people being treated for alcohol only (and no other substances) who started treatment within three weeks of referral in 2021-22

59% proportion of people being treated for alcohol only (and no other substances) leaving treatment services in 2021-22 whose treatment was successful

£637 million reported local authority spending on all drugs and alcohol treatment services in 2021-22

£533 million additional funding from central government for local authority-commissioned substance misuse treatment services 2022-23 to 2024-25, announced in December 2021

16% reduction in number of people receiving treatment services for alcohol only (and no other substances) in England between 2013-14 and 2020-21

10% increase in number of people receiving treatment services for alcohol only (and no other substances) in England between 2020-21 and 2021-22

82% the proportion of people in England estimated to be alcohol dependent that were not receiving alcohol treatment services in 2018-19

Briefing on alcohol treatment services

Background and scope

1 The safe level of alcohol consumption continues to be the subject of research and policy debate worldwide, but it is clear that excessive drinking can have costs for both society and individuals. In 2022 a member of Parliament expressed concern to the National Audit Office about the provision of alcohol treatment services in England. In this briefing we have collated some publicly available evidence on alcohol treatment services, which affect only a small number of heavy drinkers. This briefing describes:

- the background of alcohol consumption and associated harm;
- spending on, and commissioning of, alcohol treatment services; and
- access to, and outcomes from, treatment services.

2 We have held discussions with officials at the Department of Health & Social Care, NHS England and the Association of Directors of Public Health and have reviewed publicly available information. We have not audited or validated the information.

3 We recognise that a fuller consideration of alcohol harm could include an evaluation of policies, implementation and prevention. However, in the absence of a government strategy for reducing alcohol harm against which we could assess progress, we have set out in this briefing the facts about alcohol treatment services. Services in prisons are not in the scope of this work as they are commissioned by NHS England rather than local authorities.

Part One

Alcohol consumption and harm in England

1.1 Drinking alcohol is both legal and, for many, pleasurable. However, individuals who drink above low-risk levels put themselves at an increased risk of developing serious health problems and injuries, or of dying from alcohol-related causes. In England, the government estimates that around 600,000 people are dependent on alcohol.[1] The more people drink, the greater their risk of experiencing the negative health consequences of alcohol.

1.2 This part of our briefing sets out:

- trends in alcohol consumption; and
- some areas of alcohol-related harm for individuals and society.

Alcohol consumption

1.3 The Health Survey for England (HSE) 2021 presents measures of weekly consumption in line with the UK chief medical officers' (CMOs') *Low-Risk Drinking Guidelines*.[2,3] The measures are:

- lower risk (up to 14 units per week for men and women);
- increasing risk (above 14 and up to 50 units per week for men, above 14 and up to 35 units per week for women); and
- higher risk (above 50 units per week for men, above 35 units for women).

One unit of alcohol is equivalent to a half pint of regular-strength beer or half a small glass of wine.

1 According to the *NICE treatment summary on alcohol dependence*, the term 'alcohol dependence' is a cluster of behavioural, cognitive and physiological factors that typically include a strong desire to drink alcohol, tolerance to its effects and difficulties controlling its use. Someone who is alcohol-dependent may persist in drinking, despite harmful consequences, such as physical or mental health problems. The prevalence of people with alcohol dependency is calculated using a methodology developed by Sheffield University, based primarily on the adult psychiatric morbidity survey. Available at: https://bnf.nice.org.uk/treatment-summaries/alcohol-dependence/

2 NHS Digital, *Health Survey for England, 2021, part 3: Drinking alcohol*, 15 December 2022 (viewed on 1 February 2023). Available at: https://digital.nhs.uk/data-and-information/publications/statistical/health-survey-for-england/2021/part-3-drinking-alcohol

3 Department of Health and others, *UK chief medical officers' Low-Risk Drinking Guidelines*, August 2016 (viewed on 1 February 2023). Available at: https://assets.publishing.service.gov.uk/government/uploads/system/uploads/attachment_data/file/545937/UK_CMOs__report.pdf

1.4 In England, around 10 million people are estimated to regularly exceed the CMOs' low-risk guidelines, including 1.7 million who drink at higher risk. Alcohol consumption peaked in the mid-2000s and has trended downwards since then. In the HSE 2021, 21% of participants reported that they had not drunk alcohol in the last 12 months. The proportion of people who do not drink is typically higher in younger age groups than older age groups. In the HSE 2021, 38% of 16- to 24-year-olds reported that they had not drunk alcohol in the last 12 months compared with 15% of 55- to 74-year-olds. The proportion of adults reporting that they drank on five or more days in the previous week was 11%. This figure was higher for older age groups than younger, at 18% for those over the age of 55 compared with 3% of 16- to 24-year-olds. The proportion of adults drinking more than 14 units per week has been generally falling since 2011. A lower proportion of adults aged 16 to 64 reported drinking above low-risk levels in 2021 than in 2011; for those aged 65 and over, the proportion was higher (**Figure 1** overleaf).

1.5 The Office for Health Improvement and Disparities (OHID) published a series of annual estimates on the number of adults who were alcohol dependent and potentially in need of specialist treatment, based on NICE guidelines.[4] It estimated that approximately 602,000 adults experienced alcohol dependence severe enough to require specialist treatment in 2018-19, the most recent year for which data are available.[5]

Alcohol-related harm

1.6 The total number of deaths in England from conditions that were wholly attributable to alcohol has been generally rising since 2001 but has risen sharply since 2019. In 2020, the number of deaths that were wholly attributed to alcohol rose by 20% from 5,820 in 2019 to 6,984, with a further rise of 8% to 7,558 in 2021. Between 2001 and 2021, it rose by 89% (**Figure 2** on page 9). Public Health England (PHE) attributed the upward trend in alcohol-specific deaths in England in 2020 to increases in alcoholic liver disease.[6] In 2021, PHE said that alcoholic liver disease had accounted for 80% of total alcohol-specific deaths in England in 2020. We outline the impact of the COVID-19 pandemic and deaths from alcoholic liver disease below (paragraph 1.10 and Figure 6).

1.7 **Figure 3** on page 10 shows that alcohol mortality from conditions wholly attributed to alcohol in the most deprived socio-economic quintile is more than double that of the least deprived quintile. In 2020, there were 19 deaths per 100,000 persons in the most deprived quintile compared with nine per 100,000 persons in the least deprived.

4 These estimates were previously published by Public Health England until it was disbanded in October 2021.
5 The 602,000 figure was a central estimate with a lower bound (95% confidence interval) of 494,000 and an upper bound (95% confidence interval) of 761,000.
6 Public Health England, *Monitoring alcohol consumption and harm during the COVID-19 pandemic*, July 2021 (viewed on 9 February 2023). Available at: www.gov.uk/government/publications/alcohol-consumption-and-harm-during-the-covid-19-pandemic

Figure 1

Proportion of adults reporting in the Health Survey for England that their estimated weekly alcohol consumption was more than 14 units per week, by age group, 2011 to 2021

The percentage of adults drinking over the chief medical officers' current upper threshold for low-risk drinking between 2011 and 2021 fell from 26% to 21%

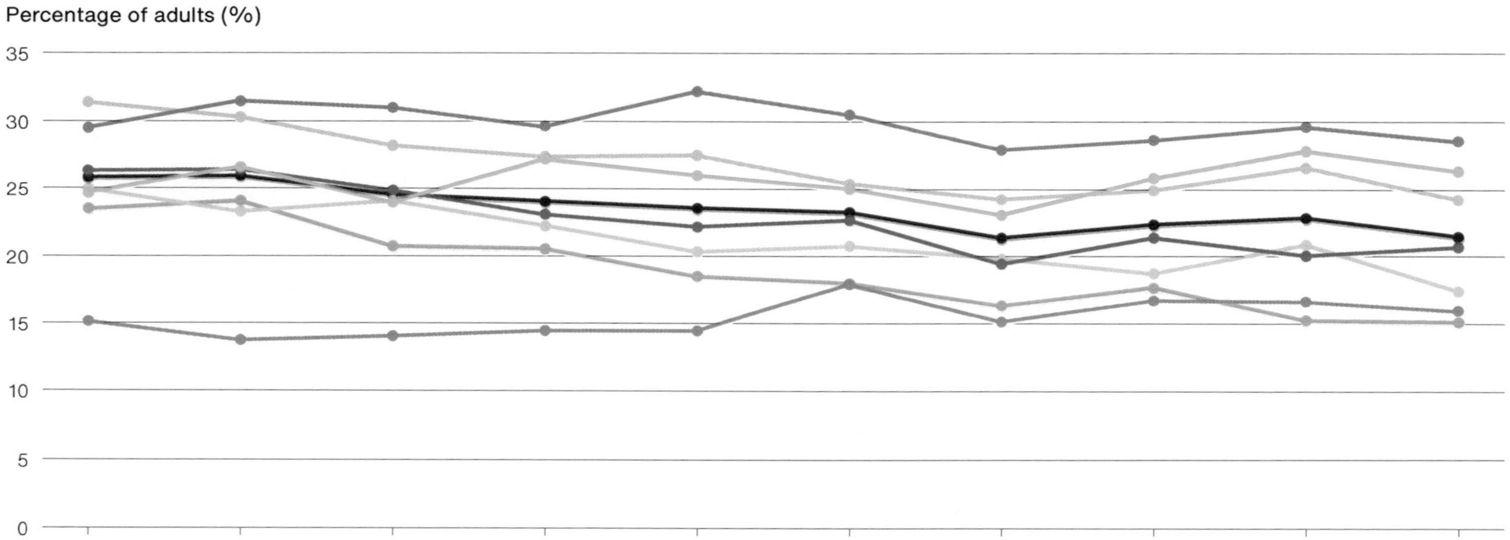

	2011	2012	2013	2014	2015	2016	2017	2018	2019	2021
All ages	**25.7**	**25.8**	**24.4**	**23.9**	**23.4**	**23.1**	**21.2**	**22.2**	**22.7**	**21.3**
16–24 years	23.3	23.9	20.6	20.4	18.4	17.9	16.2	17.6	15.1	15.0
25–34 years	24.8	23.1	23.9	22.1	20.2	20.6	19.7	18.6	20.7	17.3
35–44 years	26.2	26.3	24.7	22.9	22.0	22.5	19.3	21.2	19.9	20.5
45–54 years	31.3	30.2	28.1	27.3	27.4	25.3	24.1	24.8	26.5	24.1
55–64 years	29.4	31.4	30.9	29.5	32.1	30.4	27.8	28.5	29.5	28.4
65–74 years	24.5	26.5	23.8	27.1	25.9	24.9	22.9	25.7	27.7	26.2
75+ years	15.0	13.6	13.9	14.3	14.3	17.8	15.0	16.6	16.5	15.8

Notes

1 The UK chief medical officers' upper threshold for low-risk alcohol consumption is 14 units of alcohol per week for men and women.

2 Due to a change in methodology in 2021, 2021 data are not directly comparable with previous estimates.

3 Data are not available for the Health Survey England 2020 because NHS Digital paused fieldwork due to COVID-19 pandemic-related restrictions.

4 The Health Survey for England utilises a sample population in its surveys. A total of 5,880 adults were interviewed in the 2021 survey.

Source: National Audit Office analysis of NHS Digital's Health Survey for England

Figure 2

Number of deaths in England wholly attributed to alcohol, 2001 to 2021

The number of deaths from conditions wholly attributed to alcohol has been generally increasing since 2001 but has risen sharply since 2019

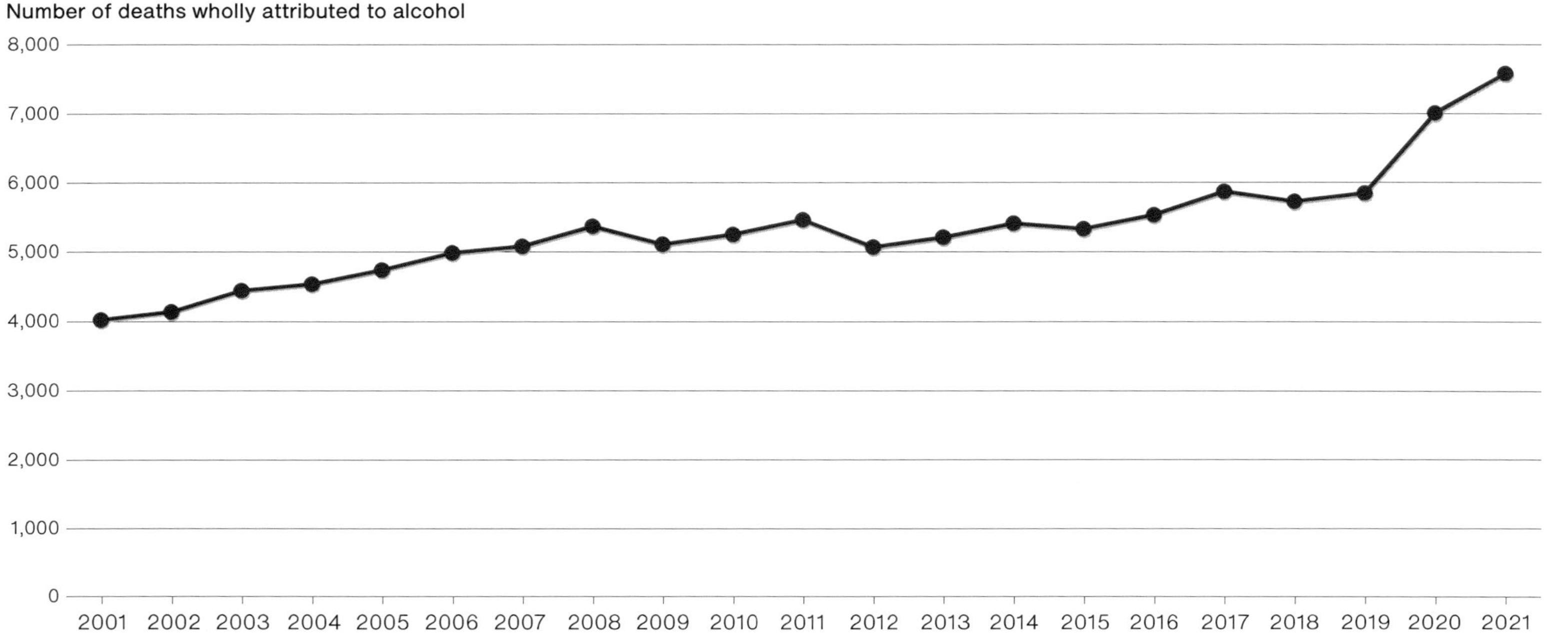

	2001	2002	2003	2004	2005	2006	2007	2008	2009	2010	2011	2012	2013	2014	2015	2016	2017	2018	2019	2020	2021
■ Deaths wholly attributed to alcohol	4,003	4,115	4,424	4,516	4,717	4,961	5,053	5,345	5,083	5,223	5,436	5,043	5,184	5,386	5,306	5,507	5,843	5,698	5,820	6,984	7,558

Note

1 Deaths that are wholly attributed to alcohol arise from conditions caused entirely by alcohol and include: alcohol-related liver disease; mental health and behavioural disorders due to alcohol; and alcohol poisoning.

Source: National Audit Office analysis of Office for National Statistics alcohol-specific deaths data for England, 2021

Figure 3

Deaths in England from conditions wholly attributed to alcohol per 100,000 persons in 2020, by deprivation quintile

Deaths in the most deprived quintile were more than double that of the least deprived quintile

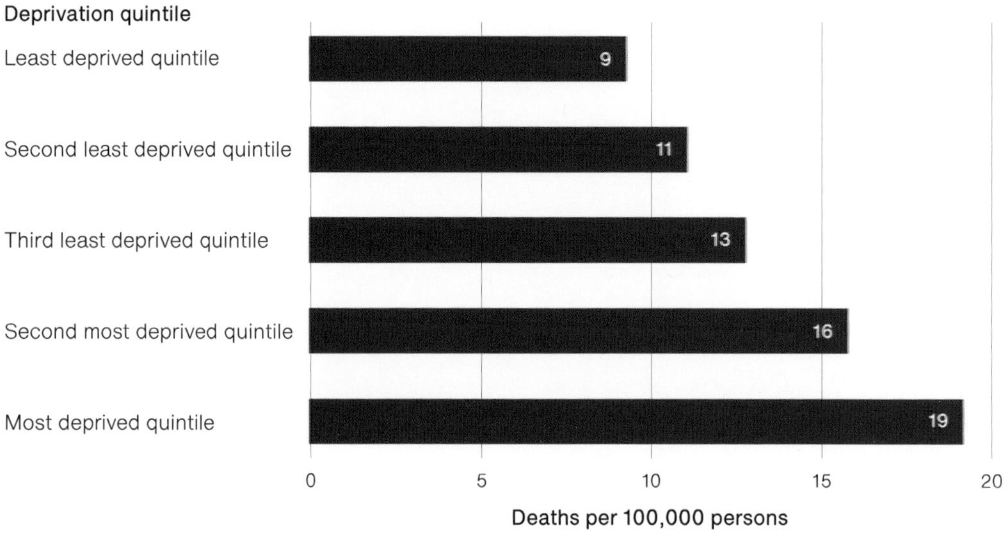

Notes

1 Deprivation deciles are defined using the Index of Multiple Deprivation 2019 local authority scores. Deprivation deciles are created by ranking upper tier local authorities in England from most to least deprived and dividing these into 10 categories with roughly equal numbers of local authorities in each. A quintile is a term in statistics that divides data in five equal groups each containing 20% of the original data.

2 These data were downloaded from the Local Alcohol Profiles for England website. The original data were split by decile.

3 To get data into quintiles we averaged each pair of deciles. For example, to get the third least deprived quintile we averaged the 5th and 6th decile from the original data.

4 Deaths that are wholly attributable to alcohol arise from conditions caused entirely by alcohol and include: alcohol-related liver disease; mental health and behavioural disorders due to alcohol; and alcohol poisoning.

Source: National Audit Office analysis of Local Alcohol Profiles for England data, 2020

Trends in alcohol harm

1.8 The total number of alcohol-related hospital admissions per year in England increased by 16% (134,662) over the four years to 2019-20, reaching just over 976,000. Over the same period, the number of hospital admissions for which alcohol was the primary reason for admission increased by more than 8% (21,281) to exceed 280,000. In line with all hospital admissions, these rates then fell sharply during the COVID-19 pandemic (**Figure 4**).

Figure 4

The number of alcohol-related hospital admissions per year in England compared with the number of total hospital admissions for all conditions, 2016-17 to 2020-21

The number of hospital admissions where alcohol was the primary reason for admission increased by more than 8% between 2016-17 and 2019-20

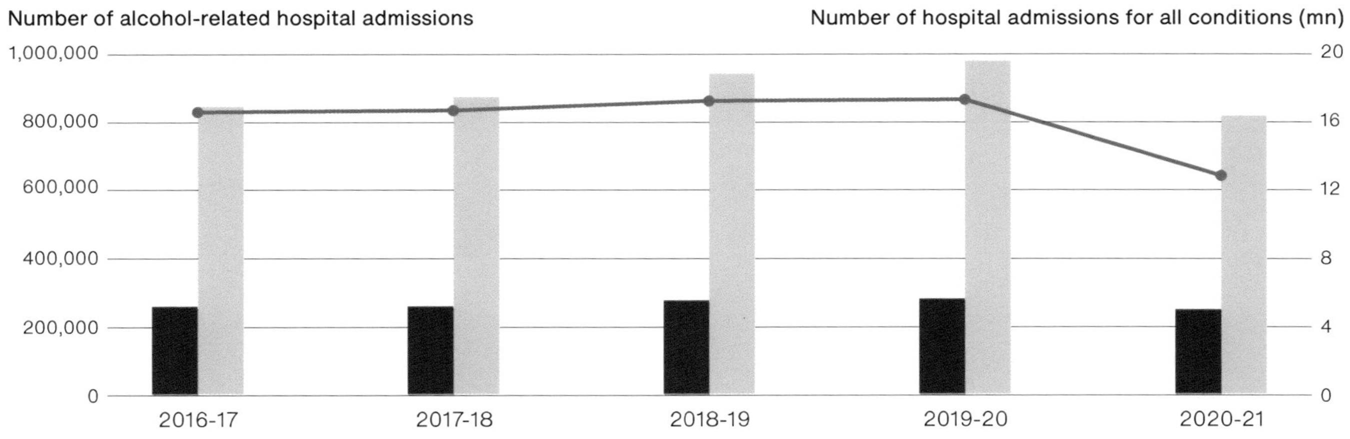

	2016-17	2017-18	2018-19	2019-20	2020-21
■ Number of admissions where the primary diagnosis is an alcohol-related condition	258,903	259,174	274,580	280,184	247,972
■ Number of admissions where the primary diagnosis or one of the secondary diagnoses is an alcohol-related condition	841,761	870,083	938,623	976,423	814,595
● Number of hospital admissions for all conditions	16,546,667	16,622,939	17,127,498	17,202,558	12,813,120

Notes

1 The number of admissions is not equivalent to the number of patients. A single patient can be admitted multiple times.

2 The data on alcohol-related admissions include conditions that are wholly attributable to alcohol (for example, acute intoxication, alcoholic liver disease and alcohol poisoning) and conditions which are partially attributed to alcohol (for example, hypertensive diseases, unspecified liver disease and unintentional injuries).

3 Data for the number of hospital admissions for all conditions were taken from NHS Digital and show the number of finished admission episodes per year.

4 In its report, *Monitoring alcohol consumption and harm during the COVID-19 pandemic*, July 2021, (viewed 1 February 2023, available at: https://assets.publishing.service.gov.uk/government/uploads/system/uploads/attachment_data/file/1002627/Alcohol_and_COVID_report.pdf), Public Health England noted a rapid decrease in the rate of alcohol-specific admissions (those wholly attributable to alcohol) coinciding with the start of the pandemic (around February 2020) and that all unplanned admissions, irrespective of their cause, sharply decreased as the pandemic started.

Source: National Audit Office analysis of Local Alcohol Profiles for England data 2016–2020 and NHS Digital hospital admissions statistics 2020-21

1.9 There are regional variations across England in the proportion of alcohol-related hospital admissions, with the north experiencing more admissions per 100,000 than the south. In 2019-20, the rate of hospital admissions where either the primary or secondary diagnoses were attributed to alcohol was 2,288 per 100,000 persons in the North East of England. This compares with 1,558 in the South East of England and 1,607 in the East of England. We have shown data for 2019-20 as the last representative year before the COVID-19 pandemic when, as we explain above, all hospital admissions fell (including those for alcohol-related conditions) (**Figure 5**). There is a similar pattern in the rate of deaths wholly attributed to alcohol (alcohol-specific mortalities). In 2020-21, the rate of alcohol-specific deaths was 20 per 100,000 persons in the North East compared with 9.93 in London and 9.25 in the East of England.

Figure 5

Hospital admissions for conditions either wholly or partially attributed to alcohol per 100,000 persons by region in England, 2019-20

The North East has the highest rate of hospital admissions for conditions either wholly or partially attributed to alcohol

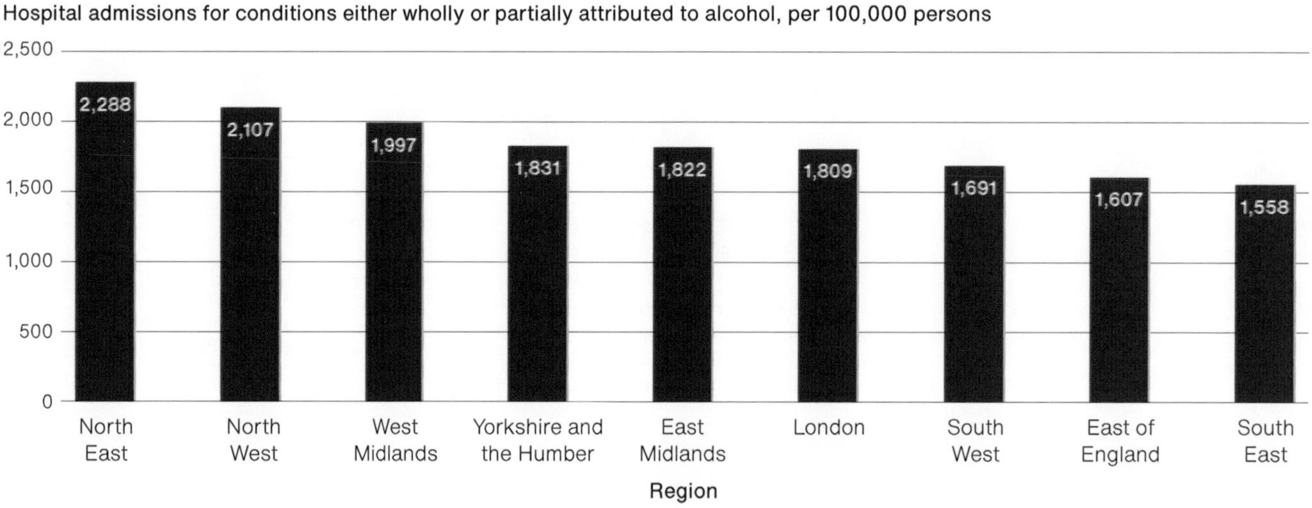

Notes

1 These data show hospital admissions where either the primary diagnosis (main reason for admission) or one of the secondary diagnoses is an alcohol-related condition.

2 Examples of conditions that are wholly attributable to alcohol include alcohol-related liver disease, mental and behavioural disorders due to alcohol, and alcohol poisoning. Examples of conditions that are partially attributable to alcohol include cancers, hypertension, cardiovascular disease.

3 We have shown data for 2019-20 as the last representative year before the COVID-19 pandemic when all hospital admissions fell (including those for alcohol-related conditions).

Source: National Audit Office analysis of Local Alcohol Profiles for England, 2020

COVID-19

1.10 In 2021, PHE reported on the changes to alcohol consumption and harms during the COVID-19 pandemic.[7] The surveys conducted as part of this research showed a sharp increase in what PHE considered riskier drinking levels in the early phases of the pandemic. PHE observed rapid decreases in the rate of alcohol-specific admissions during the pandemic. It thought these were likely to be due to people avoiding hospitals for fear of catching COVID-19 and in trying to ease pressure on the NHS. PHE concluded that alcohol-related hospital admissions and deaths had been increasing prior to the pandemic and that changes to consumption patterns during the pandemic seemed to have accelerated these trends. A similar pattern is evident in the case of deaths from alcoholic liver disease, which had been increasing steadily since 2012, then dipped before the pandemic before rising sharply (21%) in 2020 compared with 2019 (**Figure 6** overleaf). PHE reported that liver mortality rates respond quickly to changes in alcohol consumption and particularly to changes in drinking patterns of heavy drinkers, such as those seen during the pandemic.

Wider harms

1.11 Alcohol misuse results in a significant cost to the NHS in England. In 2012, the then Department of Health estimated the annual cost of alcohol harm to the NHS at approximately £3.5 billion per year. It also has a cost to wider society, through health impacts, crime and lost productivity.[8] In 2012 the Department of Health estimated the annual cost of alcohol-related harms was around £21 billion, broken down as:

- £11 billion from alcohol-related crime;
- £7 billion from lost productivity through unemployment and sickness; and
- £3.5 billion to the NHS.

1.12 The harms arising from alcohol misuse can have a significant impact on the children and family of the person misusing alcohol. In 2019, the Children's Commissioner estimated that 472,000 children lived in families where an adult reported drug and/or alcohol dependency. Parental alcohol misuse can put children at risk of abuse or neglect, and can negatively impact their health, behaviour and educational outcomes.

1.13 Alcohol misuse can also result in violent crime, although recorded rates have fallen in recent years. In 2015-16, the percentage of violent incidents where the victim believed the offender(s) to be under the influence of alcohol had fallen to a 10-year low of 39% in the most recent analysis for the period 2006 to 2016.

7 See footnote 6.
8 House of Commons, *Health Select Committee: Written evidence from the Department of Health*, July 2012. (viewed on 1 February 2023). Available at: https://publications.parliament.uk/pa/cm201213/cmselect/cmhealth/132/132we02.htm

Figure 6

Deaths from alcoholic liver disease in England, 2001–2021

Deaths from alcoholic liver disease increased 21% in 2020 compared with 2019, from 4,644 to 5,606

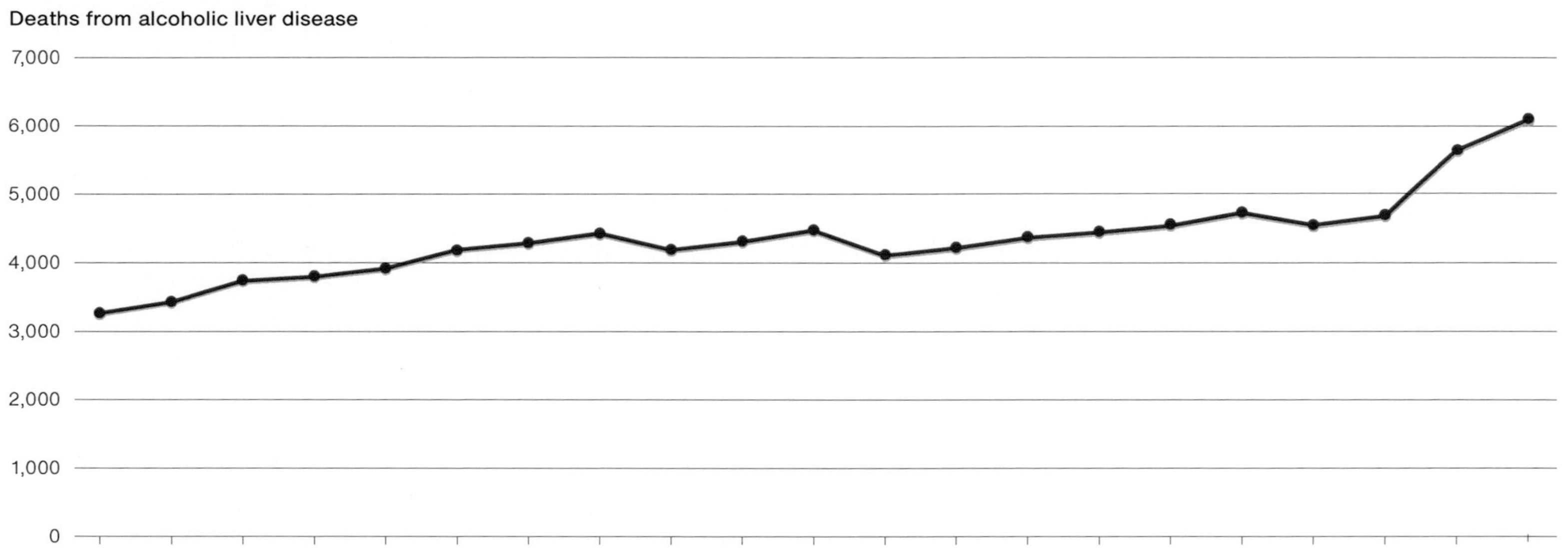

	2001	2002	2003	2004	2005	2006	2007	2008	2009	2010	2011	2012	2013	2014	2015	2016	2017	2018	2019	2020	2021
● Deaths from alcoholic liver disease	3,239	3,401	3,706	3,768	3,884	4,159	4,257	4,402	4,158	4,278	4,445	4,080	4,190	4,333	4,411	4,506	4,694	4,513	4,644	5,606	6,060

Note

1 Alcoholic liver disease refers to liver damage caused by excess alcohol intake.

Source: National Audit Office analysis of Office for National Statistics data, 2021

Part Two

Spending on, and commissioning of, alcohol treatment services

2.1 While most adults do not regularly drink to excess, according to the Health Survey for England 2021, an estimated 21% drink in a way that could risk their long-term health.[9] A minority are dependent on alcohol or are drinking at higher-risk levels and some of these seek support through alcohol treatment services. This part of our report outlines:

- the responsibilities of different parties in setting policy and commissioning of alcohol treatment services;
- spending on alcohol treatment services; and
- recent commitments from central government of additional funds for alcohol treatment services.

2.2 Addressing the full spectrum of alcohol harm described in the previous section is beyond the scope of this briefing. Our focus is on local authority-commissioned alcohol treatment services rather than any wider government response.

Roles and responsibilities

2.3 The Department of Health & Social Care (DHSC) is responsible for setting strategy and designing legislation to articulate what the public health system as a whole is aiming to achieve. This involves leading on developing national strategy and policy on tackling alcohol and drug misuse. There is currently no specific policy on the prevention and treatment of alcohol harm, although alcohol harm does feature in a minor way in the 10-year drug strategy announced in December 2021 (see paragraph 2.13). The government last published an *Alcohol strategy* in March 2012. In 2018 it announced plans to develop a new alcohol strategy but in 2020 said that other work to tackle alcohol harm negated the need for an alcohol strategy. **Figure 7** overleaf shows the roles and responsibilities of local and national bodies regarding alcohol treatment services.

9 This 21% reflects the percentage of adults in England drinking above the chief medical officers' low-risk guidelines (see footnote 3).

Figure 7

Roles and responsibilities for alcohol treatment services, in England 2023

Local authorities commission alcohol treatment services

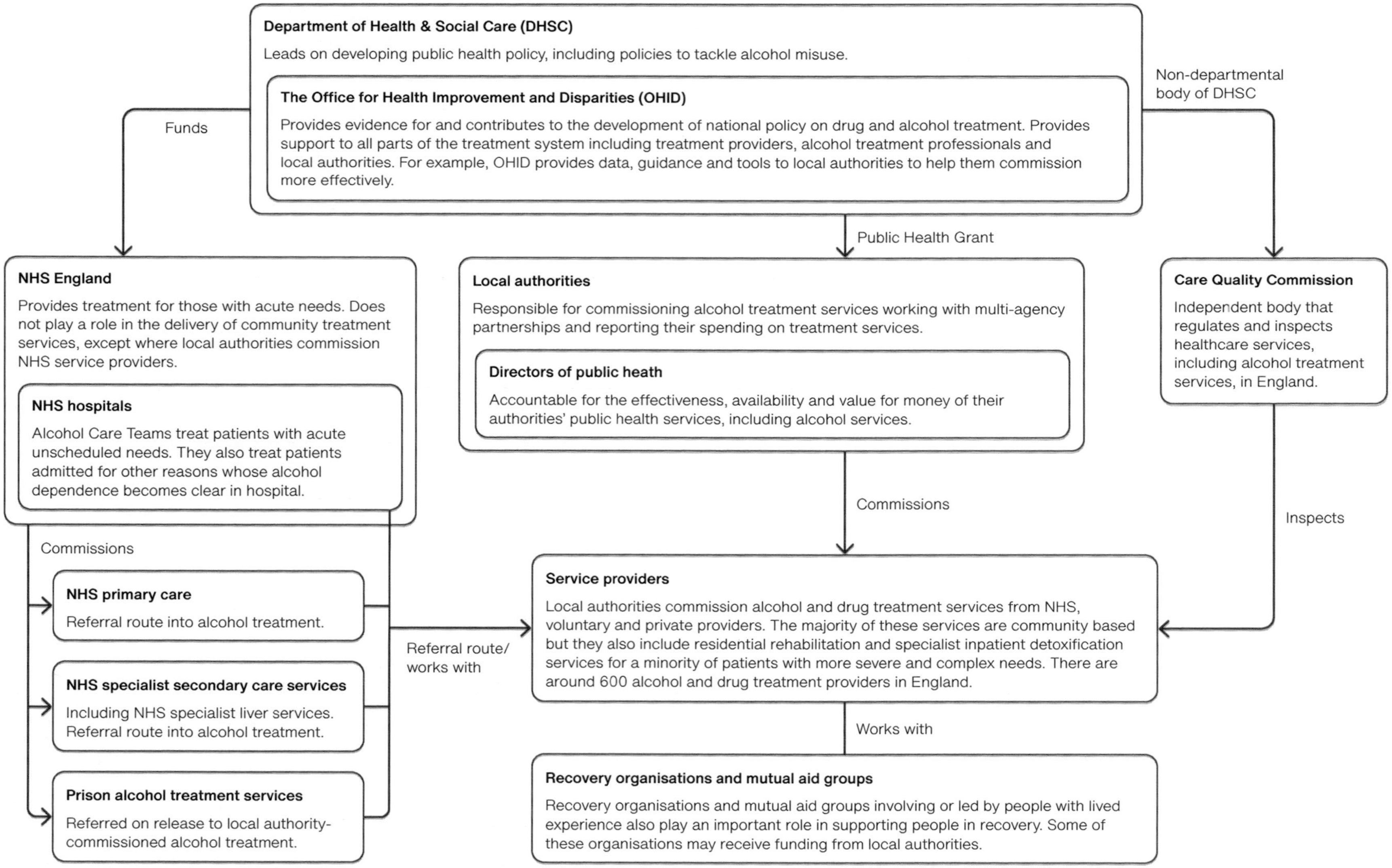

Source: National Audit Office analysis of government documents

2.4 DHSC is responsible for the allocation of the ring-fenced public health grant. Each year DHSC sets out the allocations of the public health grant between local authorities, the conditions applying to the grant, and guidance to assist local authorities. DHSC is responsible for assessing whether local authorities have met the conditions of the public health grant.

2.5 The Office for Health Improvement and Disparities (OHID) took over responsibilities relating to public health improvement from Public Health England (PHE) when it was disbanded in 2021. OHID is part of DHSC and is responsible for tackling preventable risks to health, improving the public's health and narrowing health disparities.[10] Its responsibilities include providing data, guidance, tools and support to help local authorities commission public health services more effectively. In August 2022, OHID published a commissioning quality standard (CQS) to set out the process that local authorities should follow for effective commissioning of alcohol and drug treatment and recovery services.[11]

2.6 The Health and Social Care Act of 2012 transferred responsibility for commissioning local public health services from the NHS – where primary care trusts commissioned interventions – to local authorities. Most treatment for alcohol misuse is now commissioned by local authorities. Since 2013, each local authority has a director of public health, who, using the best and most appropriate evidence, will determine the overall vision and aims for public health in their locality. They then commission the authority's public health services, including alcohol services.

2.7 Local authorities in England commission around 600 alcohol and drug treatment services from voluntary, private and NHS providers. Providers deliver most treatment services in a community setting, where people visit as outpatients, rather than a hospital or acute care setting. Local authorities can also commission residential rehabilitation and specialist inpatient detoxification services for patients with more severe and complex needs, for example in the country's seven medically managed NHS inpatient detoxification units. However, the NHS's primary remit is to deliver unscheduled acute care in hospitals. Recovery organisations and mutual aid groups involving or led by people with lived experience also play an important role in supporting people in recovery. Some of these organisations may receive funding from local authorities but the published data on local authority spending do not provide this information.

10 The Office for Health Improvement and Disparities was created within DHSC as part of the organisational reallocation of responsibilities following the abolition of Public Health England in 2021.

11 The Office for Health Improvement and Disparities, *Commissioning quality standard: alcohol and drug treatment and recovery guidance*, August 2022 (viewed on 13 February 2022). Available at: www.gov.uk/government/publications/commissioning-quality-standard-alcohol-and-drug-services

Treatment services

2.8 Local authorities commission a wide range of alcohol treatment interventions ranging from counselling and talking therapies through to prescribing medication. They also commission residential rehabilitation and specialist inpatient detoxification for a minority of people with very severe and complex needs. Local authorities commission services based on local need and priorities. NHS England, and not local authorities, commissions treatment services for people in the secure and detained estate (including prisoners). To assess local needs, the commissioning quality standard issued by OHID advises local authorities to:

- take account of local data and intelligence;
- use equality impact assessments to understand the diverse needs of local populations; and
- engage with the views of people who may benefit from support.

The type of treatment that an individual receives, and the setting in which the treatment takes place, varies depending on the extent of an individual's drinking and the complexity of their need.

2.9 In most cases, treatment provision has moved from separate alcohol and drug services to one integrated substance misuse system. In 2018, PHE published its *Inquiry into the fall in numbers of people in alcohol treatment.*[12] It reported that, of the 69 local authorities that took part in its wider consultation for the inquiry, 40 had moved to integrated services during the period of the inquiry. It indicated that 23 of the remaining authorities were already integrated before the period covered by the inquiry. The inquiry found that the main, but not only, motivation for this service re-configuration was reduced local budgets for substance misuse. We set out how local authority spending on alcohol and drug treatment services has changed in paragraph 2.17.

Funding for alcohol treatment services

2.10 Local authorities receive an annual ring-fenced grant from DHSC to help fund public health services. As a condition of the grant, government expects local authorities to improve take-up of, and outcomes from, their drug and alcohol treatment services. Since 2015-16, the public health grant has included funding for child health services, so grant figures for 2013-14 and 2014-15 are not comparable with figures for 2015-16 onwards. In 2021-22, the total public health grant was £3.32 billion compared with £3.96 billion in 2015-16 (2021-22 prices), a fall of £630 million in real terms.

12 Public Health England, *PHE inquiry into the fall in numbers of people in alcohol treatment: findings*, 2018 (viewed on 1 February 2023). Available at: www.gov.uk/government/publications/alcohol-treatment-inquiry-summary-of-findings/phe-inquiry-into-the-fall-in-numbers-of-people-in-alcohol-treatment-findings

2.11 In December 2020 the Department for Levelling Up, Housing & Communities (DLUHC) announced the Rough Sleeping Drug and Alcohol Treatment Grant (RSDATG) to deliver structured treatment and specialist support services to people who sleep rough with drug and alcohol dependency. As part of the announcement, £23 million was allocated across 43 areas in 2020-21 and up to £52 million was allocated for 2021-22 across a further 20 areas. In its September 2022 rough sleeping strategy, DLUHC announced an additional £186.5 million for the RSDATG between 2022 and 2024 spread across an additional 20 areas, bringing the total to 83 areas and five pan-London projects.

2.12 In January 2021, the government made an additional £80 million available to local authorities in England to enhance drug treatment services in 2021-22. This funding was mainly to give more support to offenders with drug and alcohol addictions by increasing the number of treatment places for prison leavers and for offenders with community sentences, with a view to cutting drug-fuelled crime.

2.13 In December 2021, in response to Dame Carol Black's independent review on drugs, the government published a new 10-year plan for tackling drug harm.[13] It outlined its vision to have a "world-class drug and alcohol treatment and recovery system across England" and committed a further £533 million over three years on top of the public health grant to "rebuild local authority-commissioned substance misuse treatment services".

2.14 From the £533 million announced in December 2021, local authorities will receive at least £80 million a year between 2022-23 and 2024-25 to spend on evidence-based interventions to: reduce drug-related death rates; bring more offenders into treatment; support the commissioning of inpatient detoxification services; and increase specialist treatment capacity for those with entrenched use and complex needs. The remaining £293 million is place-based funding aimed at reducing harm and improving recovery rates (**Figure 8** overleaf). All local authorities will receive funding over the course of the three years, but government has said it intended to prioritise places experiencing the highest harm, as determined by the rate of drug deaths, deprivation, opiate and crack cocaine prevalence, and crime. It planned to invest in the 50 local areas with the highest need in 2022-23, followed by the next 50 in 2023-24 and the final 50 in 2024-25. As part of the funding it had committed to provide, government has allocated £10 million each year for areas to commission inpatient detoxification services for drugs and alcohol for 2022-23, 2023-24 and 2024-25.

13 HM government departments, *From harm to hope: A 10-year drugs plan to cut crime and save lives*, December 2021 (viewed on 13 February 2023). Available at: www.gov.uk/government/publications/from-harm-to-hope-a-10-year-drugs-plan-to-cut-crime-and-save-lives

Figure 8

Additional funding for substance misuse services set out in the 2021 drugs plan

The government allocated an additional £533 million for substance misuse services between 2022-23 and 2024-25

Funding	2022-23	2023-24	2024-25	3-year total
	(£mn)	(£mn)	(£mn)	(£mn)
Current additional funding	80	80	80	**240**
Place-based additional funding	20	81	192	**293**
Total above existing spend	**100**	**161**	**272**	**533**

Source: *From harm to hope: A 10-year drugs plan to cut crime and save lives*, 2021

2.15 In 2019, as part of *The NHS Long Term Plan*, government allocated £27 million to establish specialist Alcohol Care Teams in the 25% of hospitals with the highest rates of alcohol-specific mortality, alcohol-related hospital admissions and deprivation. Alcohol Care Teams are primarily funded by NHS England and some are partly funded by local authorities. Alcohol Care Teams provide specialist interventions for patients in hospital with acute intoxication or other alcohol-related complications.

Local authority spending on drug and alcohol services

2.16 Within their public health grant allocation, local authorities determine their local priorities for spending. In 2021-22, local authorities reported spending a total of £4.21 billion (2021-22 prices) on public health services. This included £879 million (2021-22 prices) on COVID-19-related services. Over the period from 2016-17 to 2021-22, local authority spending on non-COVID-19-related public health services fell by £560 million (14%) from £3.9 billion to £3.34 billion (2021-22 prices).

2.17 Local authority spending on alcohol and drug services fell in the six years to 2020-21, then rose in 2021-22. In 2021-22, local authorities reported spending £637 million on alcohol and drug services. In real terms, this is a fall of 27% compared with 2014-15, when local authority spending on drug and alcohol services peaked at £873 million (2021-22 prices) (**Figure 9** overleaf). Local authorities reported spending more on drug than alcohol services in the nine years to 2021-22. In the data, local authorities separate out reported spending on drug and alcohol services. However, Dame Carol Black's 2020 report on drugs did not separate local authority spending on drugs and alcohol because, it explained, it had not been possible to disaggregate the two accurately due to a lack of robustness in reported expenditure data.[14] While recognising these cautions on the precise accuracy of the split between spending on alcohol and drugs treatment, we have disaggregated reported spending on treatment services in Figure 9 to give a sense of change over time as reported by local authorities themselves.

2.18 There is also wide variation in the reported spending on alcohol treatment services between local authorities (**Figure 10** on page 23). Local authority spending on alcohol treatment services ranged from £4,000 per 100,000 people to £1.12 million per 100,000 people in 2021-22. Three local authorities reported spending zero on alcohol treatment services.

14 Dame Carol Black, *Review of drugs: phase one report evidence pack*, February 2020 (viewed on 1 February 2023). Available at: www.gov.uk/government/publications/review-of-drugs-phase-one-report

Figure 9
Total reported local authority spending on drug and alcohol services in England between 2013-14 and 2021-22

Local authorities' reported spending on drug and alcohol services fell by 27% in real terms between peak spending in 2014-15 and 2021-22

Total local authority spending on drug and alcohol services (£mn)

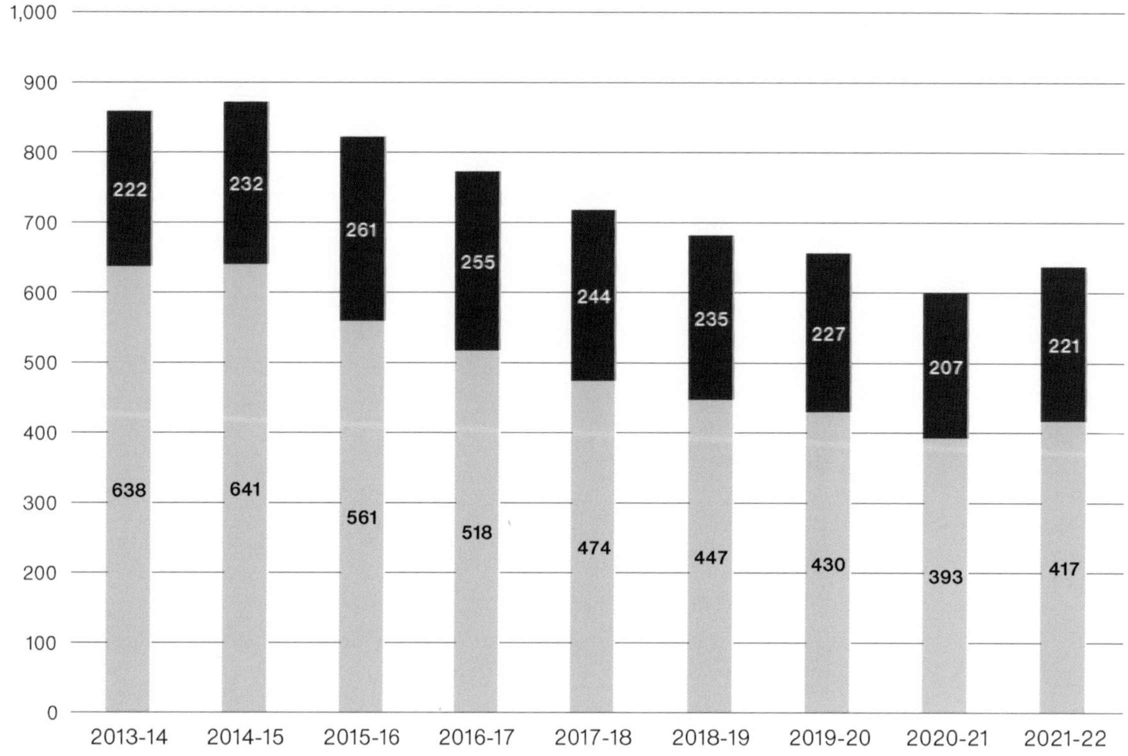

■ Total local authority spending on adult alcohol services

■ Total local authority spending on adult drug services

Notes

1 These data only contain spending on adult drug and alcohol services.

2 These data show net current expenditure on drug and alcohol services.

3 These data include spending on both treatment and prevention services. Prior to 2016-17, these categories were disclosed as a single amount but they are now disclosed separately in local authority spending returns.

4 Data have been adjusted to 2021-22 values using GDP deflator data published by HM Treasury in December 2022.

5 The data for 2021-22 include additional funding of £80 million for drug treatment in England.

6 Data have been rounded to the nearest £ million.

Source: National Audit Office analysis of local authority revenue outturn data, 2013-14 to 2021-22

Figure 10

Reported spending by upper tier local authority on adult alcohol treatment services in 2021-22 per 100,000 people

Median local authority spending on alcohol treatment services was £313,000 per 100,000 people

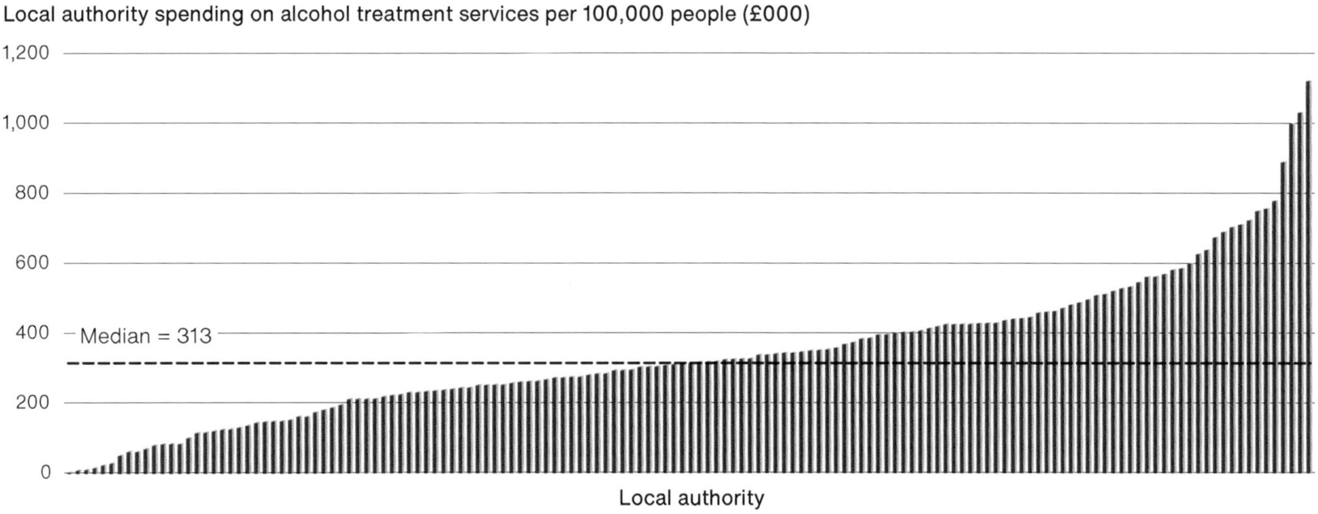

Notes

1 Spend data are taken from 2021-22 revenue outturn data.

2 Local authority population data are taken from Office for National Statistics mid-year estimates for population.

3 As of December 2022, there are 152 upper tier local authorities. This figure comprises 150 local authorities. Three of these local authorities reported spending £0 on alcohol treatment services. The source data contained no input for two local authorities: Barking and Dagenham, and Kingston upon Thames.

Source: National Audit Office analysis of local authority revenue outturn data, 2021-22

Part Three

Access to and outcomes from treatment

3.1 This part of the briefing presents data from the National Drug Treatment Monitoring System (NDTMS) on numbers of people in treatment for alcohol addiction in England and on treatment outcomes.[15] Unless otherwise stated, the data presented in this section cover those patients who are categorised into the 'alcohol only' substance group in the NDTMS data, meaning they are being treated for problems with alcohol and no other substances such as opiates or non-opiates.[16]

The people using alcohol treatment services

3.2 The number of people receiving treatment for problems with alcohol has been trending downwards since 2013-14; it increased slightly in 2020-21 and further in 2021-22. Between 2013-14 and 2020-21, the total number of people receiving treatment for problems with alcohol fell by 16% from 91,651 to 76,740. In 2021-22 the number rose to 84,697, a 10% increase from 2020-21. In 2021-22 there were 56,995 new patients, an increase of 9% from 52,220 in 2020-21, but 12% lower than the 65,110 in 2013-14 (**Figure 11**). Of the patients starting treatment in 2021-22, 60% were men and 51% were aged 30–49, with 9% aged 18–29 and 39% aged over 50. Of these new patients, 92% were white, 4% were asian, 2% were black, 2% were mixed, and 1% were other ethnic background. These figures do not include people being treated for problems with drug and alcohol misuse concurrently.[17] In 2021-22, a further 34,378 people in England were in treatment for both drug (non-opiate) and alcohol misuse, up from 28,871 in 2013-14. In the same year, a further 140,558 people in England were in treatment for opiate drugs (down from 155,852 in 2013-14), which includes people who also misuse alcohol.

15 The National Drugs Treatment Monitoring System (NDTMS) collects data from the circa 600 sites providing drug and alcohol treatment interventions across England. Treatment providers include community-based drug and alcohol services, specialist outpatient services, GP surgeries, residential rehabilitation centres and inpatient units.

16 The NDTMS shows the number of people in contact with specialist substance misuse services. People may access treatment for drug use, alcohol, or both, depending on which substance they cite as problematic at the start of treatment. Categories are: OPIATE, NON-OPIATE ONLY, NON-OPIATE and ALCOHOL and ALCOHOL ONLY. Any users mentioning opiate use would be categorised under OPIATES, irrespective of what other substances they use. Opiates include heroin and codeine, and non-opiate drugs include cannabis, cocaine and crack cocaine, ecstasy/MDMA, ketamine, amphetamines, steroids and novel psychoactive substances such as Spice.

17 See footnote 16.

Figure 11

Number of people using treatment services presenting with alcohol only treatment need, in England, 2013-14 to 2021-22

The total number of people using treatment services has been trending downwards since 2013-14 with a slight increase in 2020-21 and a further rise of 10% in 2021-22

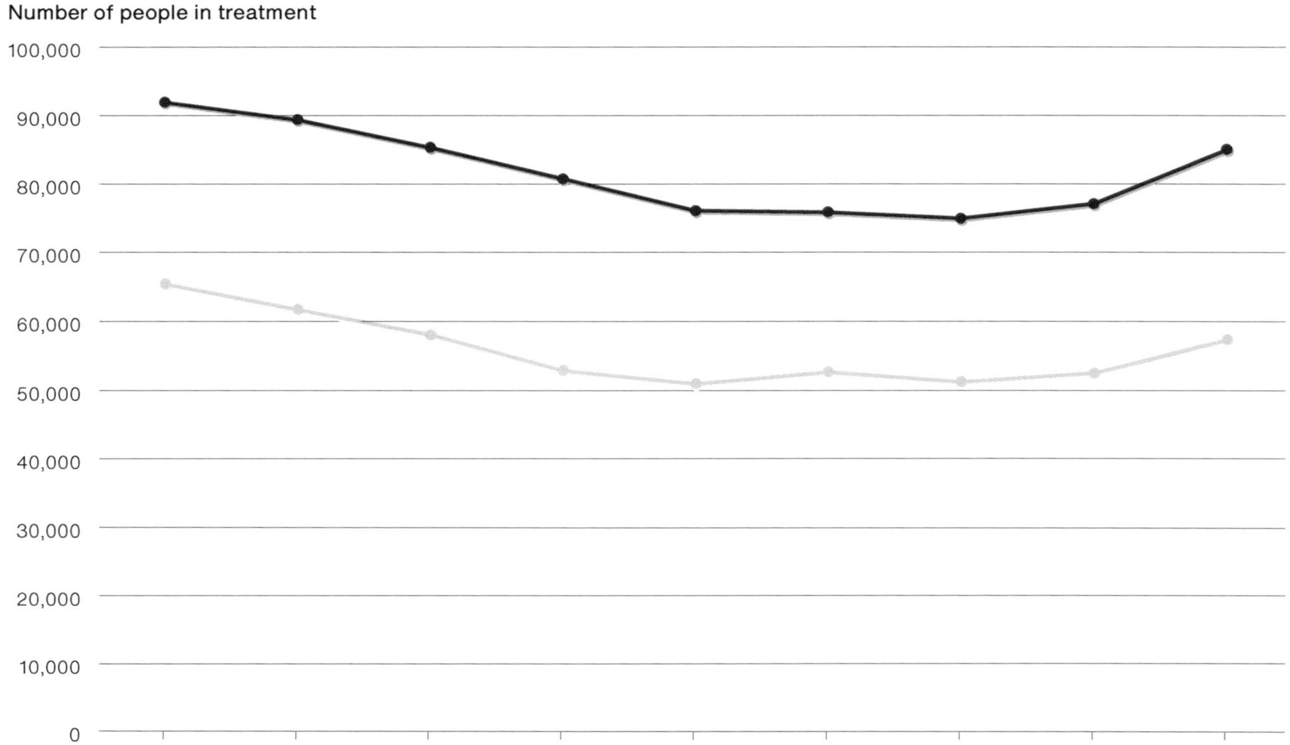

	2013-14	2014-15	2015-16	2016-17	2017-18	2018-19	2019-20	2020-21	2021-22
● Total number of people in treatment	91,651	89,107	85,035	80,454	75,787	75,555	74,618	76,740	84,697
● New entrants into treatment	65,110	61,404	57,723	52,583	50,656	52,393	50,957	52,220	56,995

Note

1 The National Drug Treatment Monitoring System divides people in treatment into substance groups. In this figure we have reported the numbers of those in the 'alcohol only' substance group, which comprises those who have problems with alcohol but do not have problems with any other substances. This means there are people receiving treatment for problems with alcohol alongside other substances who are not included in these numbers.

Source: National Audit Office analysis of National Drug Treatment Monitoring System adult data, from 2013-14 to 2021-22

3.3 Most people estimated to be alcohol dependent are not in treatment. In 2018-19, in the 151 local authorities who reported this data, a median of 18% of people estimated to be alcohol dependent were in treatment. This means that some 82% of the population considered to be alcohol dependent were not in treatment. The percentage of people estimated to be alcohol dependent but not being in treatment varies by local authority from a minimum of 58% to a maximum of 93% **(Figure 12)**.

3.4 In its 2018 report, *Inquiry into the fall in numbers of people in alcohol treatment*, Public Health England (PHE) investigated the reasons for the decline in the number of people using alcohol treatment services.[18] PHE reported that the context in which treatment was being commissioned and provided at the time, including financial pressures and service reconfiguration, had affected alcohol treatment more than treatment numbers for other substances. The report said that alcohol treatment can be delivered effectively by integrated substance misuse services. However, it said that by integrating their drug and alcohol services into a single substance misuse service, local authorities with sharp falls in numbers had generated some unintended consequences including:

- a loss of focus on the specific needs of alcohol users;
- a prioritisation of limited resources on opioid substitute treatment;
- barriers to alcohol users approaching the service, including a perception that the service focused on the needs of drug users;
- barriers to alcohol users engaging in treatment after initial contact, including a lack of alcohol-specific treatment pathways within integrated services and a loss of alcohol-specific expertise among staff; and
- referral pathways and multi-agency working that had become less effective.

3.5 PHE's report found that other factors that contributed to the fall in the number of people using alcohol treatment services included:

- reduced capacity in wider local health and social care services;
- early intervention preventing peoples' problems escalating to a point where they need treatment for dependence; and
- poor data quality.

18 Public Health England, *Inquiry into the fall in numbers of people in alcohol treatment*, November 2018 (viewed on 1 February 2023). Available at: www.gov.uk/government/publications/alcohol-treatment-inquiry-summary-of-findings/phe-inquiry-into-the-fall-in-numbers-of-people-in-alcohol-treatment-findings

Figure 12

Number of people in alcohol treatment services compared with estimated number of people with alcohol dependency and in need of treatment by upper tier local authority, 2018-19

In 2018-19 the median take-up of treatment services was 18%

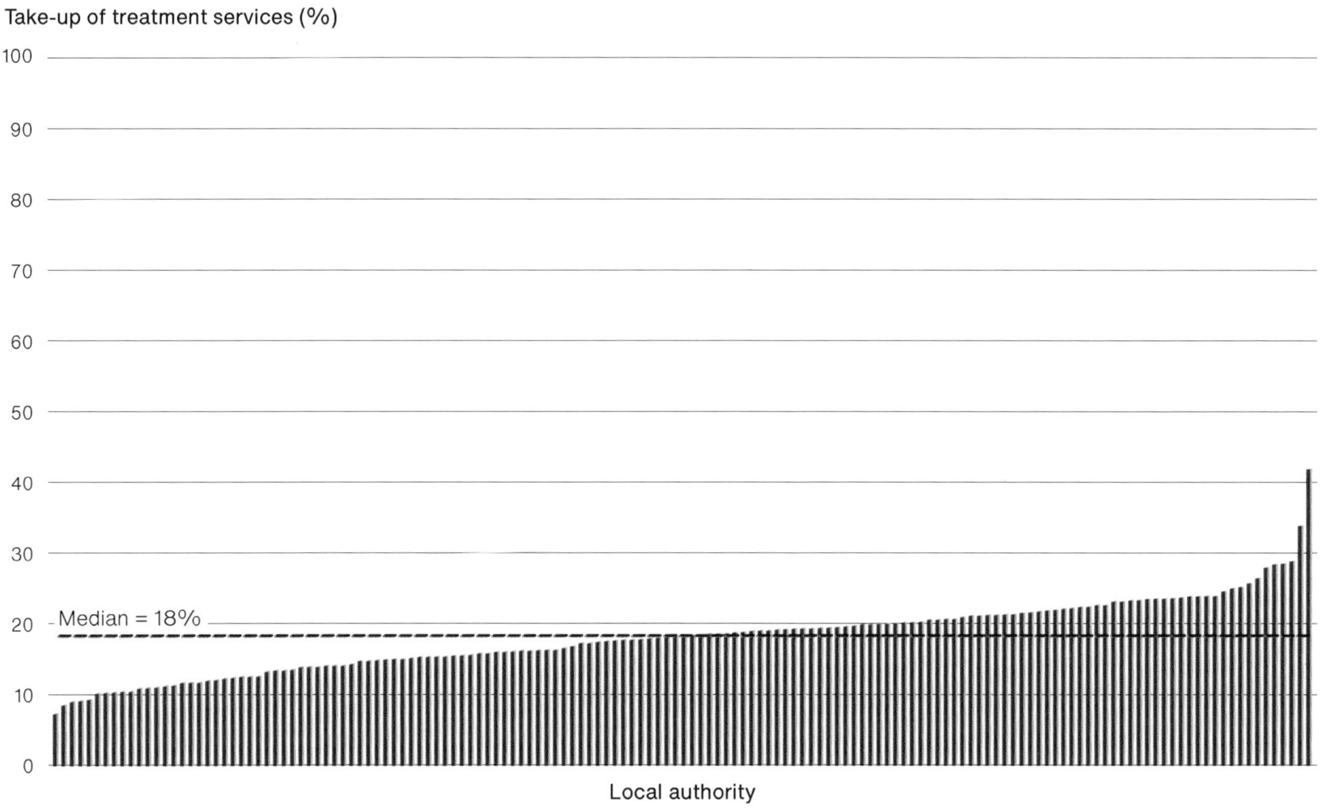

Notes

1. Data on the number of people in treatment are taken from the National Drug Treatment Monitoring System database. These data are for those in the alcohol only substance group, and alcohol and non-opiate substance group.
2. Estimates for the number of alcohol dependent people in need of treatment are taken from datasets published by Public Health England. The research for this was undertaken by the University of Sheffield. The most recent publication of these data was in March 2021 and made estimates for 2018-19.
3. In December 2018 there were 152 upper tier local authorities. This population comprises 151 upper tier local authorities. The original dataset on the number of alcohol dependent people combined the upper tier local authorities of the Isles of Scilly and Cornwall.

Source: National Audit Office analysis of National Drug Treatment Monitoring System adult data, and Public Health England alcohol dependency data, 2018-19

Treatment types

3.6 In the NDTMS data, treatments for alcohol dependence are classified by the intervention type and the setting in which the intervention is delivered. Interventions are grouped into psychosocial, such as talking therapies, and pharmacological, such as prescribing for detoxification. Settings are divided into community-based, inpatient, residential, primary care and recovery house. The data for 2021-22 show that more than 99% of people in treatment for alcohol only problems received a psychosocial intervention and 16% received a prescribing intervention. Patients can receive treatment in multiple settings: 98% of patients received treatment in a community-based setting, 4% in an inpatient setting, 2% in a residential setting and 1% in a primary care setting.

Referral routes and waiting times

3.7 Referral routes into alcohol treatment include self-referral, referral from health and social care services, substance misuse services and criminal justice services. In 2021-22, 62% of referrals came from the individual or their family and friends (**Figure 13**).[19] An individual may choose to self-refer if they feel uncomfortable speaking to their GP but would still like to receive help.

3.8 In 2021-22, 98% of people who started treatment for alcohol problems did so within three weeks of their referral, and only 1% waited for more than six weeks, although this varied by local authority. For example, in Devon 32% started treatment within three weeks and 47% waited for more than six weeks.

19 This refers to the percentage of referrals where referral source is known.

Figure 13

Referral sources for people starting alcohol treatment in 2021-22, in England

The majority of referrals came from self, family and friends, followed by health services and social care

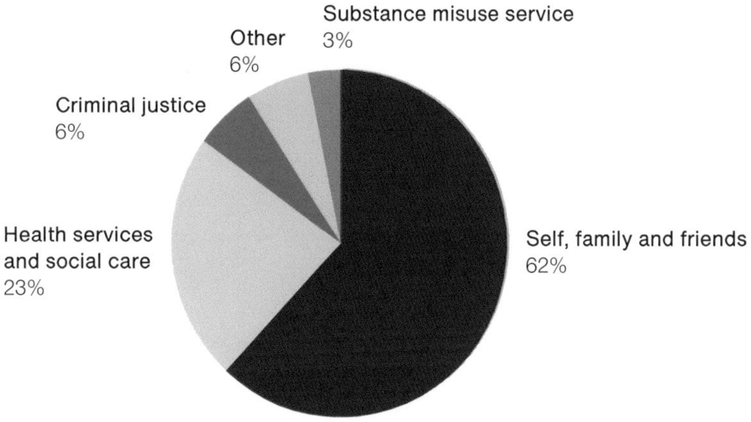

Notes

1 This figure covers those referred to treatment services who are categorised into the alcohol only substance group, which is for people with problems with alcohol and no other substances.

2 The total number of people referred to treatment services in 2021-22 in the alcohol only substance group (where referral source is known) is 56,808.

3 'Other' includes helplines and websites, employer, looked-after children, education/employment service, connexions, other, sex worker project, other young person's substance misuse service and job centre plus.

Source: National Audit Office analysis of National Drug Treatment Monitoring System adult data, 2021-22

Treatment outcomes

3.9 The NDTMS data show that the most common reason for patients leaving treatment is because it has been successful and they are no longer dependent on alcohol. Other reasons for leaving treatment include dropping out, death, transferring to another provider and treatment withdrawal. In 2021-22, 59% of patients left treatment because they had successfully completed it, 33% dropped out, and 3% transferred (**Figure 14** overleaf). For those who successfully completed treatment in 2021-22, the average treatment duration was 201 days.

Figure 14

Outcomes for those leaving alcohol treatment services in England, in 2021-22

The most common reason people left treatment was due to successful completion (59%) followed by dropping out (33%)

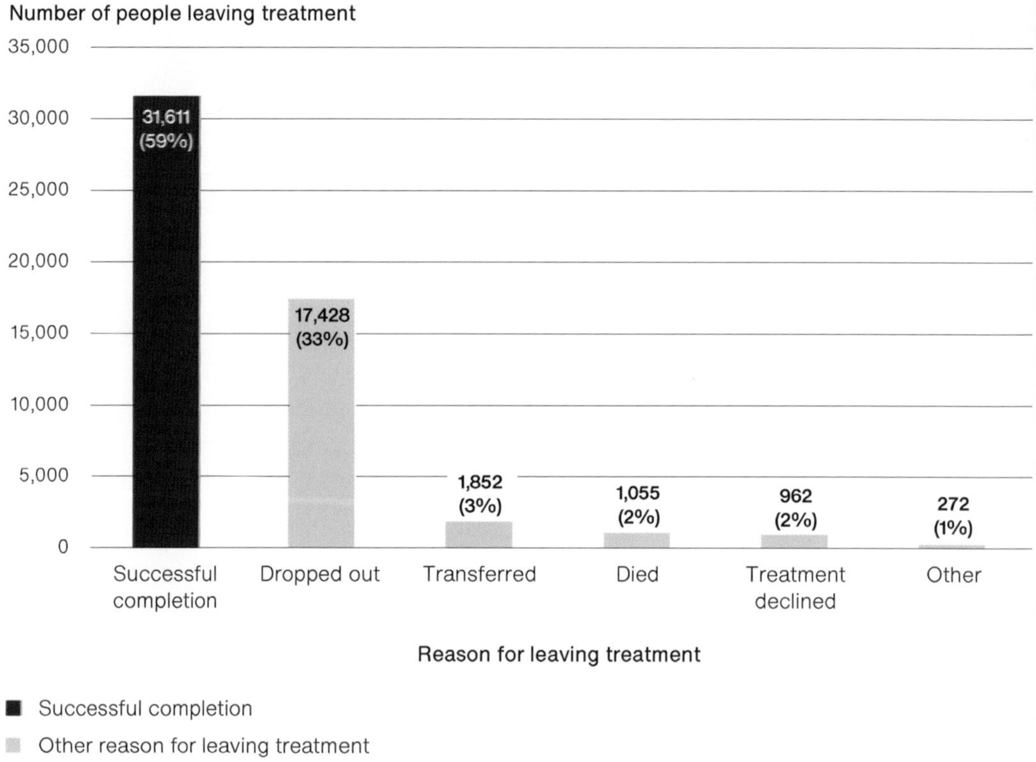

Notes

1 Successful completion of treatment is where the patient is free of alcohol dependence. 'Other' includes: moved away, no appropriate treatment, not known, prison, referred on, treatment withdrawn, inconsistent and other. 'Transferred' includes those who have finished treatment at current provider and have been referred to an alternative non-prison provider to continue their treatment. 'Transferred' also includes those who have received a custodial sentence or are on remand and a continuation of structured drug and/or alcohol treatment has been arranged at a prison provider.

2 The total population of those that left alcohol treatment services in 2021-22 was 53,180.

3 This figure covers those who are categorised into the alcohol only substance group, which is for people with problems with alcohol and no other substances.

Source: National Audit Office analysis of National Drug Treatment Monitoring System adult data, 2021-22

3.10 The Office for Health Improvement and Disparities (OHID) collects data on the change in self-reported number of days that patients used alcohol between the start of treatment and six months after starting treatment. Those using alcohol reported that they used alcohol on 21.3 out of the last 28 days at the start of treatment compared with 11.9 at their six-month review.

3.11 The data show that treatment outcomes vary over time and by local area:

- The number of people successfully completing and leaving treatment fell from 36,164 in 2013-14 to 28,349 in 2020-21 and rose to 31,611 in 2021-22. However, over the period 2013-14 to 2021-22 the percentage of those leaving treatment due to successful completion has remained steady at around 60%.
- From 2013-14 to 2019-20 the number of people dying in treatment fluctuated between 709 and 817. There was a jump in 2020-21, when 1,064 people died in treatment, an increase of 44% from 2019-20. This figure remained high in 2021-22 when 1,055 died in treatment. This represents 2.0% of those who left treatment in 2021-22 and is equivalent to 1.2% of all patients in treatment. While both percentages are low, they are the second highest in the available data from 2013-14 onwards, behind 2020-21 (2.3% and 1.4% respectively).
- Treatment outcomes vary greatly by local authority (**Figure 15**). For example, the percentage of people successfully completing treatment ranges from 29% to 90%.

Figure 15
Local variation in treatment outcomes in 2021-22

Treatment outcomes and length can vary greatly by local authority

Treatment outcomes and length	Lowest rate (%)	England average (%)	Highest rate (%)
Successfully completed treatment	Sunderland (29)	59	Barnsley (90)
Dropped out of treatment	Richmond upon Thames (0)	33	Wakefield (61)
Died in treatment	28 local authorities (0)	2	6 local authorities (6)
In treatment for under a year	Kirklees (66)	86	Stoke-on-Trent (99)

Notes

1 In treatment for under a year refers to the percentage of all patients in treatment in 2021-22. Successfully completed treatment, dropped out of treatment and died in treatment refer to the percentage of those who left treatment in 2021-22.

2 The City of London and Rutland have been excluded due to their small population sizes.

3 This figure covers those who are categorised into the alcohol only substance group, which is for people with problems with alcohol and no other substances.

Source: National Audit Office analysis of National Drug Treatment Monitoring System adult data, 2021-22

Appendix One

Our audit approach

Our approach to this briefing was to draw together publicly available information. This was supplemented by discussions with stakeholders.

Our evidence base

- We **analysed** data published by the Department of Health & Social Care (DHSC), the Office for Health Improvement and Disparities (OHID), Public Health England (PHE), NHS England, the Office for National Statistics (ONS) and the Department for Levelling Up, Housing & Communities (DLUHC). The datasets we used covered waiting times for treatment, alcohol-related hospital admissions and mortalities, local variation in treatment outcomes, referral sources for treatment, treatment outcomes and local authority revenue outturn data.
- We **reviewed** the government's December 2021 drug strategy *From harm to hope: A 10-year drugs plan to cut crime and save lives*, the *Independent review of drugs by Professor Dame Carol Black* (February 2020), government's *Alcohol strategy* (2012), *The NHS Long Term Plan* (January 2019) and questions and responses in Parliament on alcohol treatment, prevention and harms.
- We **reviewed** published literature and guidance from PHE, OHID and the NHS including clinical guidance, annual reports and treatment frameworks.
- We **reviewed** briefing papers and research such as:
  - the Alcohol Health Alliance report, *It's everywhere;*
  - Public Health England research, *PHE inquiry into the fall in numbers of people in alcohol treatment: findings;* and
  - House of Commons Library summary report, *Alcohol Statistics: England.*

Printed in Great Britain
by Amazon

19907508R00020